D0892084

# Benjamin Franklin

## History Maker Bios

## Victoria Sherrow

⌐ LERNER PUBLICATIONS COMPANY • MINNEAPOLIS

*For my brother Ed, who shares Franklin's love of music*
*and would have enjoyed the Junto*

Illustrations by Tim Parlin

Text copyright © 2002 by Victoria Sherrow
Illustrations copyright © 2002 by Lerner Publications Company

Lerner Publications Company
A division of Lerner Publishing Group
241 First Avenue North
Minneapolis, MN 55401 U.S.A.

Website address: www.lernerbooks.com

Library of Congress Cataloging-in-Publication Data

Sherrow, Victoria.
    Benjamin Franklin / by Victoria Sherrow.
        p.    cm. — (History maker bios)
    Includes bibliographical references and index.
    Summary: Describes the life and accomplishments of Benjamin Franklin,
the American statesman, author, and inventor.
    ISBN: 0–8225–0198–8 (lib. bdg. : alk. paper)
    1. Franklin, Benjamin, 1706–1790—Juvenile literature. 2. Statesmen—
United States—Biography—Juvenile literature. 3. Inventors—United
States—Biography—Juvenile literature. 4. Printers—United States—
Biography—Juvenile literature. [1: Franklin, Benjamin, 1706–1790.
2. Statesmen. 3. Printers. 4. Scientists.] I. Title. II. Series.
    E302.6.F8 S55 2002
    973.3'092—dc21                                             2001003828

Manufactured in the United States of America
1 2 3 4 5 6 – JR – 07 06 05 04 03 02

# TABLE OF CONTENTS

INTRODUCTION 5

1. CANDLE MAKER'S SON 6

2. B. FRANKLIN, PRINTER 15

3. GREAT IDEAS 24

4. FRANKLIN FOR AMERICA 31

5. TO FRANCE FOR FREEDOM 38

TIMELINE 44

THE GLASS ARMONICA 45

FURTHER READING 46

WEBSITES 47

SELECT BIBLIOGRAPHY 47

INDEX 48

# INTRODUCTION

**B**enjamin Franklin was one of the most talented people who ever lived. He helped America grow from a group of colonies ruled by Great Britain into a free, new nation: the United States. Franklin was a writer, an inventor, a scientist, and a leader. People all over the world admired him. Yet he came from a poor family and had little schooling. All his life, Franklin worked hard to educate himself. He also worked to make America a better place to live.

This is his story.

# 1 CANDLE MAKER'S SON

A blue ball hung over the door of a small wooden house on Milk Street in Boston. In colonial American towns, it was the sign of the candle maker. Benjamin Franklin was born in that house on January 17, 1706.

The fifteenth of his father's seventeen children, Ben joined a busy household in a busy city. At that time, Boston was the largest town in America. Several thousand people lived there. Ships brought cloth, tea, and metal goods to Boston's port. They carried timber, furs, and tobacco to Europe. The sea trade made some Bostonians rich.

The Franklins were far from rich. Ben's father, Josiah, worked hard making soap and candles to support his family.

*Ben lived just blocks from Boston Harbor. The Atlantic Ocean made his street smell like sea salt.*

Josiah Franklin entertained his family by playing religious music on the violin.

When Ben was six years old, the Franklins moved to a larger home and shop on Union Street. Friends and neighbors often came to visit. Ben liked to listen to the grown-ups talk. Sometimes his father played the violin, too.

By age seven, Ben had learned to read and write. Josiah Franklin decided that his clever son should become a preacher. This meant he must get a good education. When Ben entered school at age eight, he became the best student in his class.

Then Josiah changed his mind. Ben's school cost more than the family could afford. The next year, Ben went to a different school. Math was hard for him, but he loved reading and writing.

Josiah changed his mind again. He took Ben out of school to work in his shop. There Ben cut wicks and melted animal fat to make tallow. Then he poured the tallow into molds to make candles.

The tallow used in candle making came from the fat of cows and sheep.

Ben hated making candles in the hot, smelly shop. He would much rather be at Boston Harbor, watching the big ships come and go. The idea of traveling to new places excited Ben. Maybe he could go to sea as a sailor? But his father said no.

Most of all, Ben missed going to school. He decided to teach himself by reading. The Franklins owned few books, so Ben borrowed and bought others. "All the little money that came into my hands was ever laid out in books," he remembered years

later. Late at night, he read by the light of crooked candles that his father could not sell in the store.

*Ben taught himself French, German, Italian, and Spanish.*

## AN HONEST LESSON

One day, Ben decided that he and his friends needed something to stand on as they fished for minnows. He spotted a pile of stones nearby, where a house was being built. The stones would make a perfect _wharf_, Ben thought. He talked his friends into moving the whole pile. The next day, the men working on the house tracked down their missing stones and complained. Ben argued that his idea had been clever and useful, but his father soon convinced him that "nothing was useful which was not honest."

Next to reading, Ben enjoyed being outdoors. He was a skillful swimmer and loved to go fishing and boating. His love of swimming inspired his first inventions. One day, he made a set of paddles. Strapped to his wrists and feet, the paddles helped him swim faster, but it hurt to wear them.

Ben also tried hanging on to a flying kite, which pulled him speedily across the water. Another time, he and his friend Nathan bought pieces of an old boat and made them into a new boat.

Ben still spent most of his time working in the candle shop. Then, in 1718, he agreed to become an apprentice, someone who learns a trade by working for a person who is skilled in that job. Ben's older brother James was a printer and newspaper publisher. Twelve-year-old Ben signed a paper promising to work nine years for him.

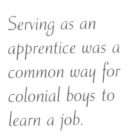

*Serving as an apprentice was a common way for colonial boys to learn a job.*

Colonial printers used a separate metal block for each letter of a book or newspaper.

James was a strict master who demanded hard work and obedience. Ben spent all day setting type, running the press, and selling newspapers. He really wanted to write for the newspaper, but would James print his writing? Ben didn't think James would want his younger brother to outshine him.

Ben came up with a plan. He wrote letters to the paper and signed them "Mrs. Silence Dogood." At night, he pushed them under the door of the printing office.

James found the articles. He didn't know who wrote them, but they were so good he published them in the paper.

Readers loved Silence Dogood. Ben's letters talked about life in Boston in both serious and funny ways. They poked fun at the British government, too.

Ben was happy to see his work in print. But James was angry when he found out who had written the Dogood letters. They argued, and Ben decided to leave. He stuffed his extra shirts and stockings into his coat pockets and boarded a ship for New York City. There, Ben Franklin planned to start a new life. At age seventeen, he was on his own.

# 2 B. FRANKLIN, PRINTER

**B**en Franklin's first weeks away from home were difficult. He could not find work in New York. So he headed for Philadelphia, Pennsylvania, one hundred miles away. Tired and dirty after the long trip, he trudged along the city streets. Pulling the last dollar from his pocket, he bought bread.

*When he arrived in Philadelphia, Ben was dirty, poorly dressed, and quite hungry.*

Luckily, Ben had a useful skill. Soon he found a job in a printing shop. He earned enough money for food, clothes, and rent.

Ben liked Philadelphia. The colony of Pennsylvania had been founded in 1682 as a place for people seeking religious freedom. Philadelphia had grown larger than Boston. Its people talked freely about religion and politics. That was fine with Ben Franklin. He loved to discuss new ideas.

About a year after he arrived in Philadelphia, Ben decided to visit Boston. He was proud to return with money in his pockets and new clothes on his back. James wouldn't make peace with him, but his parents forgave him for running away.

Ben began spending time with a cheerful, hard-working young woman named Deborah Read. Her mother ran the boardinghouse where he lived. Deborah and Ben got along well. They talked about getting married.

*Deborah Read was a carpenter's daughter. Like Ben, she had little schooling as a child.*

*In London, Ben enjoyed swimming in the Thames River. He was so skilled that he thought about opening a swimming school.*

First, Franklin had an important trip to make. The next year, 1724, he sailed to London to buy printing equipment. He spent eighteen months there, working in printing shops. Franklin went to theaters and concerts for the first time. He enjoyed meeting people who shared his many interests, but he lost touch with Deborah.

Back in Philadelphia, Franklin formed a club to keep exploring his ideas. Members of the Junto met on Friday evenings. They talked about books, politics, history, poetry, and science. And they asked questions: How could they improve themselves? How could they improve their city?

Franklin's printing business grew quickly. By 1729, at age twenty-three, he owned his own press. He began to publish a newspaper called the *Pennsylvania Gazette*. Along with printing the paper, Franklin wrote articles for it. Over time, it became the most popular newspaper in colonial America.

Ben became friendly with Deborah Read again. They married in 1730. The couple lived on Market Street above the print shop with young William, born in 1731. Francis, known as Franky, came along in 1732.

*Ben was relieved to find that Deborah still cared for him, even after their years apart.*

Deborah Franklin and her mother helped Ben run the Franklins' shop.

In a shop next door to the print shop, the Franklins sold writing supplies, books, coffee, tea, and soap. Soon Ben Franklin was the most important book dealer in Philadelphia.

Reading was still one of his greatest delights. In those days, books were costly and scarce. Franklin suggested that the Junto start a "library company." Members paid fees that were used to buy books. Anyone in the group could then borrow a book. This was America's first lending library. Other towns liked the idea and started libraries of their own.

Franklin found another way to reach readers. In 1732, he wrote an almanac. Most colonial families owned almanacs. These books contained weather predictions, recipes, poems, jokes, and advice.

Ben created a funny character named Richard Saunders for *Poor Richard's Almanac.* People enjoyed Franklin's clever writing and "Richard's" useful advice. The almanac was so popular that Franklin wrote one each year until 1758.

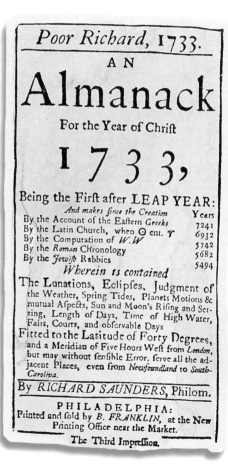

*The first POOR RICHARD'S ALMANAC sold well. In the next year's edition, Richard joked that his wife could finally afford to buy her own cooking pot instead of borrowing the neighbor's.*

## Sayings of Poor Richard

- A penny saved is a penny earned.
- The worst wheel of a cart makes the most noise.
- An ounce of prevention is worth a pound of cure.
- When the well's dry, we know the worth of water.
- The cat in gloves catches no mice.
- An apple a day keeps the doctor away.
- Well done is better than well said.
- What you seem to be, be really.
- The sleeping fox catches no poultry.
- Early to bed and early to rise makes a man healthy, wealthy, and wise.
- God helps them that helps themselves.
- Great talkers, little doers.
- Hunger never saw bad bread.
- Light purse, heavy heart.

Franklin's almanac made people laugh, but it also encouraged them to live a good life. In his own life, Franklin kept looking for ways to improve. He made a list of thirteen virtues, good qualities he wanted to achieve. They included being humble, fair, clean, and sincere. Each week, he wrote in a diary about both his successes and his failures.

Ben never became perfect, but he found that his program helped him make friends. People had always liked his sense of humor and his lively way of talking. Soon he became a better listener, too. He tried not to argue when he disagreed with people. Instead, he gently explained his own views.

Ben Franklin was happy. He was earning a good living, raising a family, and improving his mind. He found himself thinking more and more about ways to make his world a better place.

# 3 GREAT IDEAS

Around him, Ben Franklin saw much to do. For one thing, Philadelphia's streets were not paved. They grew dusty in hot weather. Then they turned muddy when it rained. Franklin paid to have one street paved as an example. The experiment was a success. People in Philadelphia agreed to pay a tax to pave all the city's streets.

Fires were another problem in the city. Franklin helped to build a volunteer firefighting team in 1736. That same year, he faced a terrible sorrow. His son Franky died of smallpox. Through his sadness, Ben continued working to help others. With the Junto, he urged people to form a police force and build new schools and a hospital.

Franklin also began to think beyond the city of Philadelphia. He became involved with Pennsylvania's government. As the clerk of the assembly, he took part in lawmaking meetings.

*Because many colonial homes and shops were made of wood, fires were a terrible danger.*

*In Franklin's time, the delivery of mail was paid for by the people who received it, not those who sent it.*

In 1737, Franklin was made postmaster for Philadelphia. At age thirty-one, he was in charge of the entire city's mail service. The post office was located next to the Franklins' home and shop. Deborah did most of the daily work there. Ben worked on improving the way mail was handled. Soon people could send letters farther and faster than ever.

Franklin found new ways to improve education, too. In 1740, he led an effort to start a school that grew into Philadelphia's first college. It later became the University of Pennsylvania.

Ben kept learning and thinking. He began to build devices to make people's lives easier. His Franklin stove, invented in 1740, fitted right into a fireplace. It did a better job of warming a room than other stoves did. Many inventors sold their creations for money. But Ben shared his with the public for free.

A few years later, the Franklins welcomed a new child into their family. Sarah, who was called Sally, was born in 1743.

*Franklin didn't name his stove after himself—a customer did. Ben had called it the "Pennsylvania fireplace."*

By 1748, Franklin was earning money from several jobs and businesses. He stopped working as a printer. The family moved to a larger home in a quieter part of Philadelphia. There Ben spent more time on science. He invented many useful things, such as a candle that burned whale oil instead of wax. It lasted longer than regular wax candles and gave more light.

Franklin studied plants, water, the weather, health and disease, animals, the stars, and dozens of other things. Of all these, he became most famous for his work with electricity. He studied this subject for years and carried out many experiments.

## A Shocking Show

Ben wasn't the only electrical pioneer of his time. In 1746, Jean-Antoine Nollet showed how electricity travels through the human body. He connected seven hundred monks to an electrical device. The shock sent the monks hopping—and King Louis XV, who was in the audience, into fits of laughter.

Ben wasn't sure that his kite experiment would work. He worked on it in secret so he wouldn't be embarrassed if it failed.

Franklin believed that lightning was an electric spark. To test this idea, he built a kite out of silk in 1752. He tied a key at the end of the kite's string. In June, he and his son William flew the kite during a storm. When lightning flashed near the kite, Franklin touched the key. He felt a shock and saw a spark. Electricity had run down the kite string. Franklin's idea was correct. Lightning really was a form of electricity!

The forty-six-year-old scientist put this information to good use. Lightning sometimes struck buildings, causing fires. Franklin placed a long, pointed metal rod on the peak of his roof. He ran a wire from the rod to the ground. If lightning struck, it hit the rod, not the house. The electricity ran down the wire and safely into the ground. "Franklin's rod," as people called it, was a huge success. From Philadelphia, it spread throughout America and Europe.

Whenever Ben Franklin saw a problem, he looked for ways to fix it. By the 1750s, new problems were growing in America. Many people had begun to be unhappy with the way their leaders in Britain were ruling them. The colonies needed people with good ideas who could get things done. Ben Franklin had proved he could do just do that.

# 4 FRANKLIN FOR AMERICA

**B**en's new challenges started in London. Beginning in 1757, Pennsylvania's government sent him there on a series of missions. His job was to convince the colony's British leaders to give Pennsylvanians more freedom.

Franklin did his best, but he didn't make much progress. Britain's king and lawmakers wanted to rule America strictly.

Next Franklin asked the British to stop taxing the colonists without their agreement. The British lawmaking assembly, Parliament, could create new taxes whether the colonists wanted to pay them or not. Americans especially wanted Parliament to end the Stamp Act. This tax was passed in 1765. It forced the colonists to buy British stamps to put on newspapers and other documents.

*Under the Stamp Act, Americans had to pay for stamps like this one for almanacs, newspapers, and even playing cards.*

Ninety thousand pounds of tea were dumped overboard in a protest that was named the Boston Tea Party.

Ben talked to many British lawmakers, explaining why the Stamp Act was unfair. He answered hours of questions for Parliament. Thanks to Franklin and other Americans, the hated tax was ended in less than a year.

Still, high taxes remained on products like tea. Then a new law forced the colonists to buy tea only from a British company. In December 1773, a group of Boston men dressed as Indians and went to the harbor. They boarded three British ships and threw their cargoes of tea overboard. Furious, Parliament closed the port of Boston and filled the city with troops.

Some colonists began to talk about fighting for independence. Like many Americans at the time, Franklin hoped things wouldn't go that far. He wanted America to remain British—but only if Britain gave the colonists more rights. He tried to convince the British to reopen Boston Harbor, but they would not.

Ben was still in Britain in February 1775 when he found out that Deborah had died. He had lost his wife of forty-four years. And he had failed to help the British and the Americans work out their differences. In March 1775, Franklin left for America, discouraged.

After closing Boston's port, Parliament forced the city's people to allow British soldiers to stay in their homes.

*Franklin oversaw the printing of America's first paper money.*

Franklin reached Philadelphia in May. By that time, fighting had begun in Massachusetts. The Revolutionary War had started. A group of men from each of the thirteen British colonies gathered in Philadelphia to decide what to do. Ben was chosen to represent Pennsylvania in this group, the Second Continental Congress.

At age sixty-nine, Ben Franklin was the oldest member of the congress. Most men his age no longer worked. But Franklin took on more jobs than he ever had before. He worked to find weapons for American soldiers. He helped the colonies print their own paper money, too.

In July 1775, the congress made Franklin postmaster of the colonies. Until this time, America had no national postal system. Ben organized a system that could deliver mail from Maine to Georgia. Mail traveling between the cities of Boston, New York, and Philadelphia arrived within a week in good weather.

For a while, the Continental Congress tried to make peace with Britain. But Britain would not grant the colonists their rights. Ben realized that fighting for independence was the only way. Most of the congress agreed.

## WILLIAM THE LOYALIST

Franklin's son William wanted the American colonies to remain loyal to Britain. People who shared this belief were called loyalists. Ben and William tried not to let their differences come between them. But their disagreement was so strong that it ended their relationship.

*Franklin was one of five men who worked on the Declaration of Independence.*

In June 1776, Thomas Jefferson began writing a document to declare the colonies free from British rule. Franklin read his work and suggested a few changes. The Continental Congress approved the Declaration of Independence on July 4, 1776. The colonies were now a new nation, the United States of America.

Ben's next big job would take him back across the Atlantic Ocean. The Americans were losing the war. They needed help. So the Continental Congress sent Franklin and two other men to France in October 1776. There they would try to save America's fight for freedom.

# 5 To France for Freedom

In France, seventy-year-old Ben Franklin found many admirers. The French regarded him as a great scientist. They liked his charming manners. In his simple fur cap, spectacles, and plain clothing, he stood out among the richly dressed French who welcomed him.

Franklin told everyone who would listen about the American fight for freedom. French generals agreed to help train American troops. Other French gave money for the struggle. And in 1778, France and the United States signed a treaty. Now the French sent money, supplies, soldiers, and guns.

*Ben became so popular in France that ladies wore lightning-rod hats to honor him.*

*Ben's bifocal glasses helped him read and see better over distances.*

For more than eight years, Franklin stayed in Paris to keep France's support. As always, his mind was busy with new projects. In about 1783, he invented bifocals—a new kind of eyeglasses that helped people see better.

With the help of the French, America won the Revolutionary War at last. In 1783, Franklin helped to write a peace treaty with Britain. It was called the Treaty of Paris. He also made treaties between the United States and other countries in Europe. But Franklin was eager to return home. He left France in 1785 after Thomas Jefferson came to replace him.

Back in America, Ben Franklin was hailed as a hero. He was elected to lead the state of Pennsylvania. He also joined other American leaders in approving and signing the United States Constitution in 1787. This document described the way the American government would work.

At age eighty-one, Ben Franklin was the Constitution's oldest signer. An elderly man, he began to experience poor health. But he still enjoyed his grandchildren, friends, and home—especially his books.

*Ben approved the Constitution even though he didn't agree with every part of it. "I expect no better," he said, "and I am not sure that it is not the best."*

He also continued to speak his mind. During his lifetime, he had owned some slaves. Now he realized slavery was wrong. Near the end of his life, he wrote articles against slavery and became president of a group that hoped to end it.

Franklin died in 1790 at age eighty-four. He was buried beside Deborah. More than twenty thousand people came to his funeral.

## FRANKLIN'S WILL

In the will he wrote before his death, Franklin left a walking stick to George Washington. To his daughter, Sarah, he willed a diamond-framed portrait of the king of France. He also set up charity funds for the cities of Philadelphia and Boston and forgave a debt owed to him by his son-in-law, Richard Bache. (In return, Franklin asked that Bache set free his slave, a man named Bob.) To his loyalist son, William, Ben left just a small farm in Canada.

*One of Franklin's last acts was to send a petition against slavery to Congress.*

Thomas Jefferson, America's third president, called Benjamin Franklin "the greatest man and ornament of the age and country in which he lived." But throughout his life, Franklin thought of himself as a common person. This belief was shown on his tombstone. He asked that it be engraved with these simple words: "Benjamin and Deborah Franklin, 1790."

# TIMELINE

BENJAMIN FRANKLIN
WAS BORN ON
JANUARY 17, 1706

## In the year . . .

1716   Ben began working in his father's candle-making shop.

1718   he became an apprentice for his brother James, a printer.    Age 12

1723   he ran away to Philadelphia and began working as a printer.

1730   he married Deborah Read.    Age 24

1731   he helped organize America's first library.

1732   he wrote the first *Poor Richard's Almanac.*

1736   he helped form a volunteer firefighting team in Philadelphia.

1740   he helped start a school that became the University of Pennsylvania.    Age 34
he invented the Franklin stove.

1752   he proved that lightning was a form of electricity.

1766   he helped convince the British Parliament to cancel the Stamp Act.    Age 60

1773   the Boston Tea Party took place.

1775   the Revolutionary War began.
he became postmaster of the American colonies.

1776   he helped Thomas Jefferson write the Declaration of Independence.    Age 70

1778   he convinced the French to help America fight for its freedom.

1783   the Revolutionary War ended with victory for America.    Age 77

1787   he signed the United States Constitution.

1790   he died in Philadelphia on April 17.    Age 84

*44*

# THE GLASS ARMONICA

Have you ever made music by rubbing wet fingers around the rim of a glass? If so, you might like one of Benjamin Franklin's most unusual inventions. The glass armonica was made of thirty-seven glasses set in a case. The player pressed a foot pedal to make the glasses turn. With wet fingers, the player touched the rims of the glasses, creating sweet, ghostly music. The glass armonica became quite popular. The great composers

Mozart and Beethoven wrote music for it. Unfortunately, players found that the turning glasses hurt their hands, and the instrument lost popularity. Still, Ben wrote that of all his inventions, this one gave him the most pleasure.

# FURTHER READING

NONFICTION
Edwards, Pamela Duncan. *The Boston Tea Party.* East
Rutherford, NJ: Penguin Putnam, 2001. A rhythmic
retelling of this pivotal event in colonial history,
accompanied by illustrations.

January, Brendan. *The Revolutionary War.* New York:
Children's Press, 2000. A photo-illustrated overview of the
American Revolution.

Moore, Kay. *If You Lived at the Time of the American
Revolution.* New York: Scholastic, 1998. Answers questions
about what life was like, especially for children, during the
Revolutionary War.

Noll, Cheryl Kirk. *The Ben Franklin Book of Easy and
Incredible Experiments.* New York: John Wiley and Sons,
1995. A hands-on journey through many of Franklin's
scientific interests, including musical instruments,
electricity, and weather.

FICTION
Fleming, Candace. *The Hatmaker's Sign: A Story by
Benjamin Franklin.* New York: Orchard Books, 1998. Two
stories in one, this picture book describes how Franklin told
an amusing tale to soothe Thomas Jefferson's hurt feelings
as Congress made changes to the draft of the Declaration of
Independence.

Lawson, Robert. *Ben and Me.* Boston: Little, Brown & Co.,
1988. A humorous retelling of Franklin's accomplishments
by a mouse named Amos, who takes credit for almost all
of them.

# WEBSITES

**Benjamin Franklin's Autobiography**
<earlyamerica.com/lives/franklin/index.html> The story of
Franklin's early life in his own words.

**The Electric Franklin**
<www.ushistory.org/franklin/index.htm> This treasury of
Franklin material includes quotes, games, a biography, the
Silence Dogood articles, and more.

**The World of Benjamin Franklin**
<www.fi.edu/franklin/rotten.html> A biography of Franklin
that focuses on his many careers and interests. Includes a
family tree and a list of books and websites.

# SELECT BIBLIOGRAPHY

Brands, H. W. *The First American: The Life and Times of
Benjamin Franklin.* New York: Doubleday, 2000.

Commager, Henry Steele, and Richard B. Morris, eds. *The
Spirit of Seventy-Six: The Story of the American Revolution
as Told by Participants.* New York: Crown, 1983.

Franklin, Benjamin. *The Autobiography of Benjamin
Franklin.* New York: Dover Books, 1986.

Lopez, Claude-Anne, and Eugenia W. Herbert. *The Private
Franklin: The Man and His Family.* New York:
W. W. Norton and Company, 1975.

Van Doren, Carl. *Benjamin Franklin.* New York: Viking, 1938.

# INDEX

Apprentice, 12–14
Armonica, glass, 45

Birth, 6
Boston, 6, 7, 10, 14, 17, 33, 34, 36, 42
Boston Tea Party, 33

Candle making, 7, 9–10, 12
Constitution, 41
Continental Congress, 35–37

Declaration of Independence, 37

Education, 5, 8, 10
Electricity, 28, 29, 30

Family, 7, 19, 41
Firefighting, 25
France, 37–40
Franklin, Deborah Read, 17, 19, 20, 26, 34, 43
Franklin, Francis, 19, 25
Franklin, James, 12–14, 17
Franklin, Josiah, 7, 8–9, 11
Franklin, Sarah, 27, 42
Franklin stove, 27
Franklin, William, 19, 29, 36, 42

Glasses, bifocal, 40
Great Britain, 5, 30, 32, 36, 40

Inventor, 5, 11–12, 27, 28, 30, 40, 45

Jefferson, Thomas, 37, 40, 43
Junto, 18, 20, 25

Library, 20
Lightning, 29–30, 39
London, 18, 31

New York City, 14, 15

Personality, 23
Philadelphia, 15, 16, 18, 24–26, 28, 35, 36, 42
*Poor Richard's Almanac,* 21–23
Postmaster, 26, 36
Printer, 12–13, 16, 18, 19, 28, 35

Revolutionary War, 35–40

Scientist, 5, 28–30, 38
Slavery, 42–43
Stamp Act, 32–33

Taxes, 32

University of Pennsylvania, 26

Washington, George, 42
Writer, 5, 13–14, 19, 20

## Acknowledgments

**For photographs and artwork:** © North Wind Picture Archives, pp. 4, 7, 13, 16, 18, 20, 21, 26, 27, 32, 33, 34, 39; © Corbis Royalty Free Images, p. 8; © Bettmann/CORBIS, pp. 9, 12, 25, 29, 40, 41, 45; The Library Company of Philadelphia, pp. 10, 19; Hulton|Archive/Getty Images, pp. 17, 35; National Archives, photo no. W&C#19, p. 37; The Pennsylvania Academy of the Fine Arts, p. 43. Front cover: National Archives, photo no. W&C#65. Back cover: Corbis Royalty Free Images.

**For quoted material:** Quotations attributed to Benjamin Franklin are his exact words, taken from the following sources: pp. 10, 11, *The Autobiography of Benjamin Franklin;* p. 22, *Poor Richard's Almanac,* various editions; p. 41, Brands, H. W., *The First American: The Life and Times of Benjamin Franklin;* p. 43, Benjamin Franklin's will.